THE
ULTIMATE
FILM FANATIC'S
TRIVIA CHALLENGE

Published by Sellers Publishing, Inc.
Copyright © 2018 Sellers Publishing Inc.
Text copyright © 2018 Stacia Tolman
All rights reserved.

Sellers Publishing, Inc.
161 John Roberts Road, South Portland, Maine 04106
Visit our Web site: www.sellerspublishing.com
E-mail: rsp@rsvp.com

ISBN 13: 978-1-4162-4665-7

Managing Editor: Mary L. Baldwin
Production: Charlotte Cromwell
Design by Charlotte Cromwell

Illustration Credits:
Front cover Illustration copyright © 2018 Zakharchenko Anna/www.
shutterstock.com; background cover Illustration copyright © 2018 balabolka/
www.shutterstock.com; back cover illustration © 2018 Alhovik/www.
shutterstock.com; interior illustration © 2018 Zakharchenko Anna/www.
shutterstock.com with the following exception: p. 224 illustration © 2018
Nadia Snopek/www.shutterstock.com.

10 9 8 7 6 5 4 3 2 1

Printed and bound in the United States of America.

THE
ULTIMATE
FILM FANATIC'S
TRIVIA CHALLENGE

Hundreds of Fun Film &
Television Trivia Questions

STACIA TOLMAN

SELLERS
PUBLISHING

1 What breed of toy dog is the model for the look of the Ewoks in *Return of the Jedi*?

- Pug
- Brussels Griffon
- Pekingese
- Pomeranian

ANSWER 1: Brussels Griffon, a breed which George Lucas owned

2 Match the rotten mother to the movie she is central to:

1. Joan Crawford, played by Faye Dunaway

2. Eleanor Iselin, played by Angela Lansbury

3. Mrs. Lift, played by Anne Ramsey

4. Alice Ward, played by Melissa Leo

A. *The Manchurian Candidate*

B. *Throw Momma from a Train*

C. *The Fighter*

D. *Mommie, Dearest*

3 Who is the only posthumous Academy Award winner for Best Actor?

- Sean Connery
- Peter Finch
- Paul Newman
- Richard Burton

4 In *Game of Thrones*, how big are Daenerys' dragons full grown?

- As big as a freight car
- As big as a Boeing 747
- As big as a flying alligator
- As big as flying T. Rex

ANSWER 4: At 230 feet long and with a 210 foot wingspan, they are as big as a Boeing 747.

7

5 What is the greatest number of different roles played by the same actor in one movie?

- Three
- Seven
- Five
- Six

ANSWER 5: Eddie Murphy played seven different characters in *The Nutty Professor*.

6 Which of the following actresses has gone into raising backyard chickens?

- Tori Spelling
- Jennifer Aniston
- Julia Roberts
- All of the above

7 What is a showrunner?

ANSWER 6: All of the above. 7: Considered the top job in TV, the showrunner has been described as the top of the food chain, the person who manages the budget, attends to ratings, and protects the creative vision of the show.

8 Who is the only character on *The Simpsons* to have more than four fingers?

- Maggie
- Marge
- God
- Moe

*Between two evils,
I always pick the one
I haven't tried before.*

MAE WEST

9 Who was the first woman to anchor the nightly news?

- Barbara Walters
- Connie Chung
- Diane Sawyer
- Katie Couric

ANSWER 9: Barbara Walters for ABC, in 1976

10 Match the movie star with their side business:

1. Ashton Kutcher
2. Steve Carrell
3. Jessica Alba
4. Dan Ackroyd

A. non-toxic consumer products
B. vodka
C. investment capital firm
D. general store

11 When was the Steadicam invented?

- 1955
- 1965
- 1975
- 1980

ANSWER 11: 1975. The Steadicam allowed for moving the handheld camera without any shaking.

12 "That's what she said!"
This phrase came from what
sketch comedy show turned
box office hit?

- *Monty Python's Flying Circus*
- *Saturday Night Live*
- *The Tracey Ullman Show*
- *The Dave Chappelle Show*

ANSWER 12: Wayne's World was introduced on Saturday Night Live in 1988.

15

13 Which actor has died the most times on screen?

- Sean Bean
- Robert De Niro
- John Hurt
- Vincent Price

ANSWER 13: John Hurt, an English actor whose career in film and on stage spanned more than seven decades, is said to have died more than forty times.

14 In terms of box office returns, what has been the most successful foreign language film in the USA?

- *Life Is Beautiful* (1997)
- *Amélie* (2001)
- *La Cage aux Folles* (1978)
- *Crouching Tiger, Hidden Dragon* (2000)

15 What was the first product advertised on television?

- Bulova watches
- Maxwell House coffee
- Lucky Strike cigarettes
- Buick Century sedan

16 What does Laverne like to mix with her milk?

- Pepsi
- Ovaltine
- Cinnamon Red Hots
- Vanilla extract

ANSWER 15: Bulova watches, in 1941. **16:** Pepsi. Penny Marshall, who played Laverne DeFazio on ABC's *Laverne & Shirley*, liked the beverage combination, and so had it written into her character.

You can be a little bit darker and rougher on the stage, partly because when you're in the theater, people have come to see you, and so they kind of know what they're in for. In television, you are sort of sneaking into people's homes. So, I think you can be a little bit darker on stage.

TINA FEY

 What is the most expensive movie car ever to be sold at auction?

- The 1955 Lincoln modified into the Batmobile
- The 1968 Ford Gulf driven by Steve McQueen in *LeMans*
- James Bond's 1964 Aston Martin, driven by Sean Connery in *Goldfinger* and *Thunderball*
- The 1929 Duesenberg driven by Fred Astaire and Carol Lombard in 1934's *The Gay Divorcee*

ANSWER 17: Steve McQueen's Ford Gulf fetched $11 million.

18 On NBC's *The West Wing*, what state did President Josiah Bartlet come from?

- Florida
- Virginia
- Michigan
- New Hampshire

19 When questioned about winning a Daytime Emmy, (in addition to a Grammy, a Tony, and an Academy award), this comedian and talk-show host responded, "It still counts! Girl's gotta eat!"

- Lily Tomlin
- Whoopi Goldberg
- Goldie Hawn
- Rosie O'Donnell

ANSWER 19: Whoopi Goldberg, who has won two Daytime Emmys, one for best TV host (*The View*), and the other for her TV special on Hattie McDaniel

20 What is the best-selling movie soundtrack of all time?

- *Purple Rain* (1984)
- *Saturday Night Fever* (1977)
- *Frozen* (2013)
- *The Bodyguard* (1992)

ANSWER 20: *The Bodyguard*, starring Whitney Houston and Kevin Costner, sold 17 million copies. It featured Whitney Houston's cover of "I Will Always Love You," originally written by Dolly Parton.

23

21 What is the original meaning of the term "gaffer," the lead electrician on a film set?

ANSWER 21: A contraction of "godfather," a rustic term of respect

22 Who provided the voice of Banzai the hyena in *The Lion King*?

- Cheech Marin
- Tommy Chong
- Tom Hanks
- John Travolta

23 What emblematic actress was named California's first Artichoke Queen?

- Marilyn Monroe
- Doris Day
- Lana Turner
- Lucille Ball

In films murders are always very clean. I show how difficult it is and what a messy thing it is to kill a man.

ALFRED HITCHCOCK

24 In her *Material Girl* video, Madonna copied Marilyn Monroe's hot pink dress and gloves from what 1953 movie?

- *Gentlemen Prefer Blondes*
- *Let's Make Love*
- *The Seven Year Itch*
- *Some Like It Hot*

25 How tall is Big Bird?

- 5 feet
- 6 feet
- 7 feet
- Over 8 feet

26 Where was the set location for 2015's *The Martian*?

- Tunisia
- Jordan
- Death Valley, California
- North Dakota

ANSWER 26: Wadi Rum, Jordan. Lawrence of Arabia was also filmed there.

27 Match the actor with the animated character they voiced:

1. Eddie Murphy
2. Whoopi Goldberg
3. Samuel L. Jackson
4. Vin Diesel

A. The giant in *The Iron Giant*
B. Frozone in *Frozen*
C. Shenzi the hyena in *The Lion King*
D. Donkey in *Shrek*

28 What is the record amount of money won on a single game of *Jeopardy*?

- $55,000
- $77,000
- $112,000
- $156,000

ANSWER 28: $77,000, won by Roger Craig who was 33 years old at the time and a doctoral candidate in computer science. He still held the record as of 2017.

29 Elizabeth Taylor, wearing her famous 69-carat pear-shaped diamond around her neck, presented the Academy Award for Best Picture to what movie?

- *Midnight Cowboy*
- *Bonnie and Clyde*
- *Diamonds Are Forever*
- *In the Heat of the Night*

30 What was the first feature-length computer-animated movie?

- *Cars*
- *Toy Story*
- *The Lion King*
- *Aladdin*

31 What is the Key Art Award?

Television is a medium of entertainment which allows millions of people to laugh at the same joke at the same time and yet remain lonesome.

T.S. ELIOT

32 In NBC's hit TV show *Julia* of 1968, Diahann Carroll played a single professional mother living in the suburbs. What was her job?

- Teacher
- Nurse
- Secretary
- Reporter

ANSWER 32: Nurse

33 The directorial team Ethan and Joel Coen created a fictional character named Roderick Jaynes to be credited with what job that they actually do themselves?

- Director of Photography
- Costume Designer
- Set Designer
- Editor

ANSWER 33: Roderick Jaynes is the pseudonym for the Coen brothers' editor, who was nominated for a Best Editor Oscar for his work on *Fargo* and *No Country for Old Men*.

34 What is ALF's favorite food?

- Mice
- Fried chicken
- Cats
- Pepperidge Farm Goldfish

35 Which of the following is the only actor NOT to have written a children's book?

- Jada Pinkett Smith
- Sylvester Stallone
- Spike Lee
- Jessica Lange

36 What do stars Marilyn Monroe, Cuba Gooding Jr., Kristen Stewart, and Brad Pitt have in common?

- They are all born under the astrological sign Scorpio
- They started their careers as uncredited extras.
- They are vegetarian.
- They changed their names.

37 Match the television show with the town it is set in:

1. *The Simpsons*
2. *Buffy the Vampire Slayer*
3. *King of the Hill*
4. *Murder, She Wrote*

A. Quahog, Rhode Island
B. Sunnydale, California
C. Cabot Cove, Maine
D. Springfield, Oregon

38 When was the famous "Hollywood" sign built?

- 1909
- 1918
- 1923
- 1931

*Whatever you fear
has no power —
it is your fear that
has the power.*

OPRAH WINFREY

39 Of those listed below, which movie franchise has the most entries?

- *Halloween*
- *Star Trek*
- *James Bond*
- *Godzilla*

40 A private social club at which Ivy League institution gets Hollywood A-listers to come and celebrate with them when they name them Man of the Year or Woman of the Year?

- Yale
- Princeton
- Columbia
- Harvard

ANSWER 40: At Harvard, the Hasty Pudding Club has been honoring box office stars as their Woman of the Year since 1951, and their Man of the Year since 1967, to recognize their "lasting and impressive contribution to the world of entertainment."

41 Which future action star walked away from a Fulbright scholarship to MIT?

- Dolph Lundgren
- Vince Vaughn
- Lou Ferrigno
- Vin Diesel

42 What war movie opens with this line? "Now I want you to remember that no poor dumb bastard ever won a war by dying for his country. He won it by making the other poor dumb bastard die."

- *Patton*
- *The Green Berets*
- *Apocalypse Now*
- *Full Metal Jacket*

43 What princess from Grimm's Fairy Tales showed up at the coronation of Elsa in the 2013 Disney animated movie *Frozen*?

- Sleeping Beauty
- Snow White
- Rapunzel
- Cinderella

44 What pop singer-songwriter wrote the famous jingle for Band-Aids?

- Barry Manilow
- Neil Diamond
- Barbra Streisand
- Prince

45 What epic movie's great last line was almost censored to "Frankly, my dear, I don't give a whoop."

- *Casablanca*
- *Gone with the Wind*
- *Citizen Kane*
- *The Grapes of Wrath*

ANSWER 45: In *Gone with the Wind*, Rhett Butler, played by Clark Gable, says "Frankly, my dear, I don't give a damn," in response to Scarlett O'Hara (Vivien Leigh) asking him where she should go.

*The movies are the
only business where you
can go out front and
applaud yourself.*

WILL ROGERS

46 How much does each star on the Hollywood Walk of Fame weigh?

- 100 pounds
- 300 pounds
- 450 pounds
- 600 pounds

47 Who is the highest paid animal in show biz?

- Keiko, the killer whale in *Free Willy*
- Higgins, a mongrel from a dog shelter, most famous for playing the title role in *Benji*
- Bart, an Alaskan Kodiak bear who has appeared in numerous films
- Moose, the Crane family's Jack Russell in *Frasier*

ANSWER 47: Higgins. In addition to his role as Benji, Higgins appeared in many TV shows and movies over his fourteen-year career.

48 What is the first television sitcom to air the sound of a toilet flushing?

- *Sanford and Son*
- *All in the Family*
- *I Love Lucy*
- *Leave It to Beaver*

49 Who plays Alex, the corpse in *The Big Chill?*

- Bruce Willis
- Kevin Costner
- Jeff Goldblum
- Ken Olin

50 How did sound engineer Ben Burtt create Darth Vader's famously ominous breathing?

51 To create the look of Yoda, famed British makeup artist Stuart Freeborn combined the features of his own face with those of what other noted public figure?

- The Dalai Lama
- Albert Einstein
- Carlos Castaneda
- Charles de Gaulle

52 Who has hosted the Academy Awards ceremony the most?

- Johnny Carson
- Billy Crystal
- Bob Hope
- Jack Lemmon

ANSWER 52: Comedian Bob Hope, who hosted the event 19 times

I see only one requirement you have to have to be a director or any kind of artist: rhythm. Rhythm, for me, is everything. Without rhythm, there's no music. Without rhythm, there's no cinema. Without rhythm, there's no architecture.

ALEJANDRO GONZALEZ INARRITU

53 Which of the following is the only actor who has not played J. Edgar Hoover?

- Leonardo DiCaprio
- Billy Crudup
- Ernest Borgnine
- Matt Damon

54 How many pairs of fake feet were made for the filming of *Lord of the Rings*?

- 80
- 180
- 1800
- 18000

ANSWER 54: 1800. 3,600 bare, hairy feet were needed for the hobbits.

61

55 What *Saturday Night Live* actor was originally considered for the role of Han Solo in the first *Star Wars*?

- Chevy Chase
- Bill Murray
- Dan Ackroyd
- John Belushi

56 What public figure had a
problem with Murphy Brown's
pregnancy on *Murphy Brown*?

- Anita Bryant
- Dan Quayle
- Billy Graham
- Tammy Faye Bakker

ANSWER 56: Vice-President Dan Quayle, who called out the character's choice of having
a baby as a single mother as, "mocking the importance of fathers by bearing a child alone."

57 Who is the shortest actor to have won an Oscar?

- Richard Dreyfuss
- Al Pacino
- Dustin Hoffman
- James Cagney

ANSWER 57: James Cagney, who won an Oscar for *Yankee Doodle Dandy* in 1942. He was 5'5" tall.

58 Which western featuring a shoot-out in the middle of town was the favorite movie of Presidents Dwight Eisenhower, Ronald Reagan, and Bill Clinton?

- *True Grit*
- *High Noon*
- *The Magnificent Seven*
- *The Good, the Bad and the Ugly*

59 Of the following, which actress married the most times?

- Rue McClanahan
- Lana Turner
- Elizabeth Taylor
- Zsa Zsa Gabor

Pretending is not just play.
Pretending is imagined possibility.
Pretending, or acting, is a very
valuable life skill and we
do it all the time.

MERYL STREEP

60 Of the following, which movie star has the most children?

- Eddie Murphy
- Anthony Quinn
- Charlie Chaplin
- Kevin Costner

61 What does M*A*S*H* stand for?

ANSWER 60: Anthony Quinn, who had twelve children with three wives.

61: Mobile Army Surgical Hospital

68

62 Who is the oldest person to win an Oscar for Best Actress?

- Meryl Streep
- Katharine Hepburn
- Jessica Tandy
- Helen Mirren

ANSWER 62: Jessica Tandy, who at age eighty won the Academy Award for Best Actress for her role in *Driving Miss Daisy* (1989)

63 Which actor was *People Magazine's* first 'Sexiest Man Alive' in 1985?

- Mel Gibson
- Tom Cruise
- Harry Hamlin
- Patrick Swayze

64 What was the first toy advertised on television?

- Mr. Potato Head
- Candy Land board game
- Hula Hoop
- Magic 8 Ball

65 What kind of animal was Holly Golightly's pet in *Breakfast at Tiffany's?*

- Chihuahua
- Parakeet
- Hamster
- Cat

66 What show had the first romantic interracial kiss on network television?

- *All in the Family*
- *The Twilight Zone*
- *Star Trek*
- *The Brady Bunch*

ANSWER 66: *Star Trek.* Captain Kirk (William Shatner) kissed Uhuru (Nichelle Nichols) in 1968. Two years earlier, Sammy Davis Jr., kissed character Archie Bunker on *All In the Family*, which made great waves, but it was only on the cheek.

67 What future US President liked a movie so much he named his oil company after it?

- Lyndon Johnson
- George H. W. Bush
- George W. Bush
- Donald Trump

ANSWER 67: 1959, future president George H. W. Bush named Zapata Corporation after *Viva, Zapata!* starring Marlon Brando and Anthony Quinn, when he saw the film title on a movie marquee.

*If I didn't have my films
as an outlet for all the
different sides of me,
I'd probably be locked up.*

ANGELINA JOLIE

68 What British royal claimed that the campy musical *Rocky Horror Picture Show* had "completed her education"?

- Sarah Ferguson
- Lady Diana
- Princess Anne
- Queen Elizabeth II

69 Film director Alfred Hitchcock liked to give himself cameo appearances in his movies. Match the Hitchcockian cameo with the film it appeared in:

1. Champagne drinker at the party
2. Appears in the hallway, stares into the camera
3. Leaving the pet shop with his own terriers
4. Gets pushed in a wheelchair

A. *Topaz*
B. *The Birds*
C. *Marni*
D. *Notorious*

70 The lead singer of what band lobbied to be considered for the 1971 film adaptation of Anthony Burgess' dystopian novel *A Clockwork Orange*?

- The Beatles
- The Rolling Stones
- The Who
- The Kinks

ANSWER 70: Mick Jagger of the Rolling Stones went so far as to send in a petition for the role, which included signatures by each member of the Beatles, Anita Pallenberg, and Marianne Faithfull.

71 Who is the only actress to have played twins twice?

- Lily Tomlin
- Hayley Mills
- Lindsay Lohan
- Bette Midler

ANSWER 71: Lindsay Lohan, first as Hallie Parker and Annie James in 1998's *The Parent Trap*, and in 2007 as Aubrey Fleming and Dakota Moss in *I Know Who Killed Me*

72 Which actor lost the most weight for a role?

- Matthew McConaughey
- Jared Leto
- 50 Cent
- Natalie Portman

ANSWER 72: 50 Cent, who lost 54 pounds for his role in *Things Fall Apart*

73 What do actors Sharon Stone, Lin-Manuel Miranda, Rachel McAdams, and James Franco have in common with Amazon founder Jeff Bezos?

- They are born under the sign of Leo.
- They have all worked at McDonald's.
- They are political activists.
- They all dropped out of college.

74 What is the only X-rated movie to win an Academy Award for Best Picture?

- *Blue Valentine*
- *Midnight Cowboy*
- *Last Tango in Paris*
- *A Clockwork Orange*

*I love acting.
It is so much more
real than life.*

OSCAR WILDE

75 Of the following Latino actors, which is the only one who did not get a start on telenovelas?

- Gael Garcia Bernal
- Sofia Vergara
- Salma Hayek
- Ricardo Montalban

76 What was used in *The Wizard of Oz* to make green horses in Emerald City?

- Copper sulfate
- Lime Jell-O crystals
- Spray paint
- Chlorophyll

77 What is nunsploitation?

ANSWER 76: Lime Jell-O crystals. **77:** A genre of film which had its peak in Europe in the 1970s, which feature lurid plots set in fortress-like convents, sadistic mother superiors or lecherous priests, and mortification of the flesh. Examples are *Killer Nuns*, *The Nun and the Devil*, and *Flavia the Heretic*.

78 What two original Monty
Python cast members teamed
up for 1988's heist comedy
A Fish Called Wanda?

- John Cleese and Michael Palin
- Eric Idle and John Cleese
- Terry Gilliam and Graham
  Chapman
- Terry Jones and Eric Idle

79 Leonardo DiCaprio bought what rare movie poster for a record-breaking $690,000?

- 1927's *Metropolis*
- 1935's *The Bride of Frankenstein*
- 1933's *King Kong*
- 1931's *Dracula*

80 In *Breaking Bad,* where does Walter White keep his money?

- In a heating duct
- In a toolbox
- In a safe
- In a freezer

ANSWER 80: In a heating duct

81 Who is the voice of Fillmore, the 1960s hippie van in *Cars*?

- Jeff Bridges
- George Carlin
- John Goodman
- Tommy Chong

82 Which comic actor turned down the chance to appear with Marilyn Monroe in 1959's *Some Like It Hot*?

- Jerry Lewis
- Carl Reiner
- Dean Martin
- Bob Hope

ANSWER 82: Jerry Lewis. The role of Jerry went to Jack Lemmon, who garnered an Oscar nomination for it.

Funny is an attitude.

FLIP WILSON

83 What is Kramer's first name, on *Seinfeld*?

- Joel
- Cosmo
- Ethan
- Eli

84 In what city did Sylvester Stallone mount a 40-year retrospective show of his paintings?

- Philadelphia, Pennsylvania
- St. Petersburg, Russia
- Paris, France
- New York, New York

ANSWER 84: In 2013, the exhibit was held in St. Petersburg, Russia.

93

85 Who founded Academy of Motion Pictures Arts and Sciences?

- Thomas Edison
- Louis B. Mayer
- Douglas Fairbanks
- Jack Warner

ANSWER 85: Louis B. Mayer, founder of MGM

86 What historical character has
had the most movie portrayals?

- Adolf Hitler
- Napoleon Bonaparte
- Jesus Christ
- Abraham Lincoln

87 Who is the first woman to have won an Oscar for playing a man?

- Cate Blanchett
- Hilary Swank
- Linda Hunt
- Julie Andrews

ANSWER 87: Linda Hunt, who won Best Supporting Actress in 1982's The Year of Living Dangerously

88 What is the longest
running game show?

- *The Price Is Right*
- *Wheel of Fortune*
- *Family Feud*
- *Jeopardy*

89 What film is credited with introducing reggae music to the world?

- *The Harder They Come*
- *Rockers*
- *Babylon*
- *Land of Look Behind*

Everybody has something that chews them up and, for me, that thing was always loneliness. The cinema has the power to make you not feel lonely, even when you are.

TOM HANKS

90 How old was Laurence Fishburne when he lied about his age to get a part in *Apocalypse Now*?

- Fourteen
- Fifteen
- Sixteen
- Seventeen

91 Match the box office star to the product they endorse in Japan.

1. Madonna
2. Nicolas Cage
3. Bruce Willis
4. Arnold Schwarzenegger

A. gas stations
B. ramen noodles
C. rice beverages
D. slot machines

92 What kind of feathers adorned Cher's plumed headdress in her memorable Bob Mackie outfit at the 1986 Academy Awards?

- Rooster
- Crow
- Ostrich
- Marabou

93 Which James Bond actor had a stint as a sidewalk fire-eater?

- Sean Connery
- Timothy Dalton
- Pierce Brosnan
- Daniel Craig

94 Who played guest host of the very first episode of *Saturday Night Live*?

- Johnny Carson
- George Carlin
- Steve Martin
- Bill Cosby

95 What was the character Meathead's relationship to Archie Bunker on *All in the Family*?

- Nephew
- Barber
- Son-in-law
- Neighbor

ANSWER 95: Meathead, played by Rob Reiner, was Archie's son-in-law.

105

96 Which Hollywood breakthrough role played by a non-English speaking actor won them an Oscar?

- Penelope Cruz
- Peter Lorre
- Antonio Banderas
- Andre the Giant

Respect your efforts,
respect yourself.
Self-respect leads to self-discipline.
When you have both firmly under
your belt, that's real power.

CLINT EASTWOOD

97 Who is the only person listed below not to have taught school as they waited to make it in show biz?

- Billy Crystal
- Sylvester Stallone
- Mr. T
- Kevin Costner

ANSWER 97: Kevin Costner. Billy Crystal was a substitute teacher in Long Island; Stallone and Mr. T both taught gym.

98 What is an Academy Award statue made of?

- Solid gold
- Gold-plated nickel
- Gold-plated tin
- Gold-painted plaster

ANSWER 98: Gold-plated brittanium, which is 92% tin. In WWII, due to a metal shortage, the Oscar was plaster painted gold.

99 What sultry actress released an album of Tom Waits' covers?

- Scarlett Johannsen
- Carmen Electra
- Lindsay Lohan
- Jennifer Lopez

ANSWER 99: Scarlett Johannsen, *Anywhere, Anywhere / Lay My Head*, in 2008.

100 Match the movie star with the soap opera that started their career:

1. Brad Pitt
2. Demi Moore
3. Meg Ryan
4. Sarah Michelle Gellar

A. *General Hospital*
B. *Another World*
C. *All My Children*
D. *As the World Turns*

101 How many voting members were in the Academy of Motion Pictures Arts and Sciences in 2017?

- 3,306
- 4,886
- 5,612
- 6,687

102 Which of the following actors is the only one to not work as a bouncer prior to success on the screen?

- Bruce Willis
- Dolph Lundgren
- Vin Diesel
- Laurence Fishburne

103 Who is the first African-American to have won an Academy Award?

- Hattie McDaniel
- Butterfly McQueen
- Paul Robeson
- Lena Horne

ANSWER 103: In 1939, Hattie McDaniel won Best Supporting Actress in *Gone with the Wind.*

*You can't find any
true closeness in Hollywood
because everybody does the
fake closeness so well.*

CARRIE FISHER

 104 What kind of a pet does Leonardo DiCaprio have?

- Kinkajou
- Lemur
- Wolf
- Tortoise

ANSWER 104: A Sulcata Tortoise. They can live to be 200 years old.

105 What is the name for an intentionally placed inside joke in a movie?

- An Easter egg
- A McGuffin
- A Snickers bar
- A glass hat

 The vultures in *The Jungle Book* are patterned after what rock band?

- The Monkees
- The Beatles
- The Rolling Stones
- The Grateful Dead

ANSWER 106: The Beatles

107 In *Rocky*, as part of his training regime, what does Rocky Balboa ingest every day at 4am?

- Raw eggs
- Raw fish
- Raw steak
- Raw carrot juice

108 What was the cost of a 30-second commercial during Super Bowl 2017?

- $3 million
- $4 million
- $4.5 million
- $5 million

109 Which of the following stars can rightfully claim to be bigger than Jesus?

- Whoopi Goldberg
- Tom Cruise
- George Clooney
- Kanye West

 110 Which actor gained the most weight for a role?

- Jared Leto
- Russell Crowe
- Robert De Niro
- Vincent D'Onofrio

ANSWER 110: Vincent D'Onofrio, who put on 70 pounds for his role in *Full Metal Jacket*

The wit makes fun of other persons; the satirist makes fun of the world; the humorist makes fun of himself.

JAMES THURBER

111 Which character actor known for portraying cowboy villains won a Purple Heart for service in WWII?

- Robert Mitchum
- James Cagney
- Jason Robards
- Jack Palance

112 What famed director has as an epitaph on his gravestone, "I'm a writer, but then nobody's perfect."

- Billy Wilder
- Stanley Kubrick
- Orson Welles
- Robert Altman

113 In the French film *Breathless*, which American icon does the car thief Michel, played by Jean-Paul Belmondo, try to emulate?

- John Wayne
- Humphrey Bogart
- Edward G. Robinson
- Jimmy Stewart

ANSWER 113: Humphrey Bogart

114 Match the actor with the animated character they voiced:

1. Will Smith

2. Robin Williams

3. Tom Hanks

4. Ellen DeGeneres

A. Dory in *Finding Nemo*

B. Woody in *Toy Story*

C. Genie in *Aladdin*

D. Oscar from *Shark Tale*

115 What year did a streaker make it on air for the Oscar Awards ceremony?

- 1968
- 1970
- 1974
- 1978

ANSWER 115: 1974, when thirty-three-year-old Robert Opal interrupted David Niven's announcement for Best Picture by running naked across the stage while flashing a peace sign

116 What kind of an animal is Arthur, in PBS' long-running cartoon for children?

- A bear
- An aardvark
- A rabbit
- A monkey

117 What are dump months?

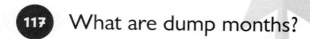

ANSWER 116: Arthur is an aardvark. **117:** The two periods of the year with the smallest movie audiences, the first being January/February, and the second August/September, when a studio might release movies with low commercial expectations, such as horror movies, and movies intended for a teen audience.

129

118 In the scandal that rocked 1958, purported mob enforcer Johnny Stompanato is stabbed in self-defense by the daughter of which major box-office star?

- Lana Turner
- Marilyn Monroe
- Carol Lombard
- Ava Gardner

ANSWER 118: Lana Turner: Stompanato's death at the hand of fourteen-year-old Cheryl Crane was ruled a "justifiable homicide."

Art is about the dynamics of the human experience.

DANNY GLOVER

119 Rather than use CGI (computer-generated imagery), how many actual squirrels did director Tim Burton use to crack nuts in *Charlie and the Chocolate Factory?*

- Twenty
- Thirty
- Forty
- Fifty

ANSWER 119: Forty. Spoiled brat Veruca Salt wants one, and the squirrels attack her, decide she's a 'bad nut,' then send her down the garbage chute.

120 What movie-turned-TV show gave Jennifer Aniston her meteoric beginning?

- *The Breakfast Club*
- *Pretty in Pink*
- *Ferris Bueller's Day Off*
- *St. Elmo's Fire*

121 In Chicago, Oprah Winfrey's Harpo Studios building was demolished in 2016 to make room for the headquarters of this fast food chain.

- McDonald's
- Burger King
- Chick Fil-A
- Wendy's

122 When asked what religion he was raised, this blockbuster movie star responded, "Democrat."

- Dustin Hoffman
- Jack Nicholson
- Harrison Ford
- Tom Cruise

123 A family once called "as important as the Kennedys," the Addams Family started out its media career as a one-panel cartoon in which publication?

- *The New Yorker*
- *Playboy*
- *TV Guide*
- *Life Magazine*

ANSWER 123: *The New Yorker* magazine. Cartoonist Charles Addams was the strip's creator.

124 Which film had the most time given to closing credits?

- *Superman*
- *Around the World in 80 Days*
- *Assassin's Creed*
- *Space Jam*

ANSWER 124: *Assassin's Creed*, in 2007, taking nearly fifteen minutes.

125 What star of countless war and cowboy epics had the given name of Marion Morrison?

- Gary Cooper
- Robert Holden
- Glenn Ford
- John Wayne

The length of a film should be directly related to the endurance of the human bladder.

ALFRED HITCHCOCK

126 Who is the only man to have won three Oscars for Best Actor?

- Tom Hanks
- Marlon Brando
- Daniel Day-Lewis
- Jack Nicholson

127 What kind of toy dog was cared for by misanthrope Melvin Udall, played by Jack Nicholson in *As Good as It Gets*?

- Pug
- Brussels Griffon
- Scottie Terrier
- King Charles Spaniel

128 What iconic and dignified actor from the silver screen era of Hollywood played Elwood P. Dowd, who talks to a 6'3" invisible rabbit named Harvey?

- Cary Grant
- Jimmy Stewart
- Spencer Tracy
- Humphrey Bogart

ANSWER 128: Jimmy Stewart, in the 1950 film, *Harvey*, which was based on a popular stage play of the same name

129 What type of business did George Jefferson, patriarch of *The Jeffersons*, own?

- Bakery
- Restaurant
- Car wash
- Dry cleaner

ANSWER 129: George Jefferson owned a chain of dry cleaning locations.

143

130 In 1981, John Hinckley attempted to assassinate President Ronald Reagan in an attempt to gain the attention of which actress he admired?

- Jane Fonda
- Jodie Foster
- Goldie Hawn
- Bo Derek

131 Which Shakespearean play has most frequently been adapted into film?

- *Romeo and Juliet*
- *As You Like It*
- *Hamlet*
- *Julius Caesar*

132 Which star was a decorated WWII bomber pilot?

- Gary Cooper
- Robert Mitchum
- Clark Gable
- Jimmy Stewart

ANSWER 132: Jimmy Stewart, who was awarded the Presidential Medal of Freedom by President Reagan, who also promoted Stewart to the rank of Major General on the U.S. Air Force Retired list

*The purpose of art
is to lay bare the questions
which have been hidden
by the answers.*

JAMES BALDWIN

133 What union does a location scout typically belong to?

- Screen Actors Guild
- American Federation of Television and Radio Artists
- The Teamsters
- International Alliance of Theatrical Stage Employees

134 Match the cameo appearance to the movie you can see it in:

1. Kareem Abdul-Jabbar
2. David Bowie
3. Billy Idol
4. Michael Jackson

A. *Men in Black II*
B. *The Wedding Singer*
C. *Airplane!*
D. *Zoolander*

135 What kind of cancer is Walter White dying from in *Breaking Bad*?

- Pancreatic
- Prostate
- Lung
- Brain

ANSWER 135: Walter White has Stage 3A inoperable lung cancer.

136 What movie used the greatest number of extras?

- *Gandhi*
- *The Last Emperor*
- *Spartacus*
- *The Ten Commandments*

137 What is a Bacon Number?

ANSWER 136: *Gandhi,* with over 300,000 used for the funeral scene.

137: The number of degrees removed a person is from actor Kevin Bacon, who did not appear in the movie *Six Degrees of Separation.* He did however claim to have worked with everyone in Hollywood, so following an article called "Kevin Bacon Is the Center of the Universe," the idea of a Bacon Number went viral.

138 Which movie uses the
f-word the most?

- *Jarhead*
- *Straight Outta Compton*
- *The Wolf of Wall Street*
- *Pulp Fiction*

ANSWER 138: *The Wolf of Wall Street* uses the f-word 569 times, for an average of 3.19 swears per minute.

139 What pop queen had a 3-minute screen appearance as a hologram in 2010's dystopian movie *The Giver*?

- Taylor Swift
- Cher
- Adele
- Beyoncé

 140 What is the most profitable movie ever made?

- *Titanic*
- *Avatar*
- *Frozen*
- *Harry Potter and the Deathly Hallows*

ANSWER 140: As of 2017, *Avatar*, with a box office profit margin of over 37%

*Comedy is acting
out optimism.*

ROBIN WILLIAMS

141 How much does it cost to have your star appear on Hollywood's Walk of Fame?

- Nothing
- $5K
- $20K
- $30K

142 Match the actor with the novel he wrote.

1. Sylvester Stallone
2. James Franco
3. Carl Reiner
4. Steve Martin

A. *Shopgirl*
B. *NNNNN*
C. *Palo Alto*
D. *Paradise Alley*

143 What is the diagnosis for Jack Nicholson's character Melvin Udall in *As Good as It Gets*?

- ADD
- OCD
- Paranoia
- Bipolar Disorder

ANSWER 143: OCD, with a pathological fear of germs.

144 Which Oscar-winning actress was a cheerleader in high school?

- Julia Roberts
- Halle Berry
- Holly Hunter
- Nicole Kidman

145 What movie closes with this line? "Roads? Where we're going, we don't need roads!"

- *Star Trek*
- *Thelma & Louise*
- *Back to the Future*
- *Harry Potter*

146 Match the name of the actor below with his original name:

1. Ice Cube
2. Ben Kingsley
3. Vin Diesel
4. Jamie Foxx

A. Krishna Bhanji
B. Marc Sinclair
C. Eric Marlon Bishop
D. O'Shea Jackson

 147 Who is the only omnivore on the following list?

- Peter Dinklage
- Ellen Page
- Ellen DeGeneres
- Johnny Depp

ANSWER 147: Johnny Depp. All the others are vegan.

Artists are the gate keepers of truth. We are civilization's radical voice.

PAUL ROBESON

148 Who is the first French actress to win an Academy Award for a French-speaking role?

- Marion Cotillard, for *La Vie en Rose*
- Catherine Deneuve, for *Indochine*
- Juliette Binoche, for *Chocolat*
- Claudette Colbert, for *It Happened One Night*

149 Who was the first ever guest star on *Sesame Street*?

- Lily Tomlin
- Johnny Cash
- James Earl Jones
- Richard Pryor

150 What is a Foley artist?

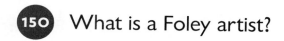

ANSWER 149: James Earl Jones, in 1969, who slowly and with great dignity recited the alphabet.
150: A Foley artist is the person who works on the sound of a film post-production, eliminating sounds and adding sounds. The job is named after Jack Foley, a radio sound man, who in the early days of talkies worked at Universal Studios.

165

151 What is the movie with the largest on-screen body count (not counting planets exploding)?

- *300*
- *Lord of the Rings: the Return of the King*
- *Troy*
- *Kingdom of Heaven*

ANSWER 151: With 836 deaths shown on screen, the highest body count goes to *Lord of the Rings: The Return of the King*

152 Match the movie to the inappropriate paternal behavior it features:

1. *American Beauty*

2. *Chinatown*

3. *Star Wars*

4. *The Shining*

A. Sires a child with his daughter

B. Obsessed with teenaged daughter's best friend

C. Attempted murder of family with ax

D. Cuts off son's hand

153 *The Simpsons* debuted as a short piece of animation on what variety show?

- *Saturday Night Live*
- *The Tracey Ullman Show*
- *The Tonight Show*
- *The Late Show*

ANSWER 153: *The Simpsons*, now in its 29th season, originally aired as a short on *The Tracey Ullman Show*.

154 In 2002, whose hair sold for $115,000?

- John Lennon
- Elvis Presley
- James Dean
- Rudolph Valentino

155 The film *Missing* was attacked upon its release in 1982 by the US State Department for misrepresenting US government involvement in political events in what country?

- Guatemala
- El Salvador
- Argentina
- Chile

Photography is truth.
The cinema is truth
twenty-four times
per second.

JEAN-LUC GODARD

156 Which famed French fashion house became the costume designer for Audrey Hepburn in 1961's *Breakfast at Tiffany's*?

- Givenchy
- Cardin
- Chanel
- Balmain

ANSWER 156: Givenchy

157 What was the first network to advertise a condom?

- ABC
- CBS
- CNN
- FOX

158 Of the following, who is the only actor not to have played Adolf Hitler?

- Alec Guinness
- Charlie Chaplin
- Anthony Hopkins
- Buster Keaton

159 Which director had an underwire bra specially designed for starlet Jane Russell in 1943's *The Outlaw* to emphasize her breasts?

- Howard Hughes
- Billy Wilder
- Alfred Hitchcock
- Preston Sturges

ANSWER 159: Howard Hughes. Jane Russell found the bra too uncomfortable to wear, and it now rests in a Hollywood museum. But the controversy it generated made the movie a hit.

175

 What is the highest-grossing
concert movie?

- *Woodstock*
- Justin Bieber, *Never Say Never*
- Madonna, *Truth or Dare*
- The Talking Heads,
  Stop Making Sense

161 Match the place with the *Star Wars* location:

1. Canary Wharf tube station, London
2. Tunisia
3. Norway
4. Del Norte County, California

A. Tatooine
B. Hoth
C. Endor
D. Imperial Base

162 Who is the first American woman to win an Academy Award for Best Director?

- Sofia Coppola
- Nora Ephron
- Barbra Streisand
- Kathryn Bigelow

*I can't believe it!
Reading and writing
actually paid off!*

MATT GROENING

163 Which actor has been nominated for a Best Actor Oscar the most times without winning?

- Bert Lancaster
- Tom Cruise
- Peter O'Toole
- Richard Burton

ANSWER 163: Peter O'Toole was nominated eight times but never won. In 2002, he eventually was presented with the Academy Honorary Award for his entire body of work.

164 Who is the most nominated actor in Academy history?

- Paul Newman
- Meryl Streep
- Bette Davis
- Jack Nicholson

ANSWER 164: With 17 nominations and 3 wins, Meryl Streep is the most awarded actor in Hollywood.

165 What was the first cartoon broadcast in color?

- *Rocky and Bullwinkle*
- *The Flintstones*
- *The Jetsons*
- *The Huckleberry Hound*

166 How many 1969 Dodge Chargers were destroyed during the seven-season run of *The Dukes of Hazzard*?

ANSWER 165: *The Jetsons.* **166:** Between 250 and 350 were destroyed, well more than one per episode.

167 Match the movie with the car that plays an important role in it:

1. *Thelma and Louise*
2. *The Blues Brothers*
3. *Days of Thunder*
4. *Back to the Future*

A. 1981 DeLorean
B. 1966 Ford Thunderbird
C. 1974 Dodge Monaco
D. 1990 Chevy Lumina

168 Which Shakespearean actor appears in both *Star Trek* and *X-Men* franchises?

- Christopher Lee
- Ian McKellen
- Patrick Stewart
- Alec Guinness

169 Who is the action hero to voice Rocky the Rhode Island Red, in *Chicken Run*, the highest-grossing stop-action movie?

- Mel Gibson
- Bruce Willis
- Arnold Schwarzenegger
- Tom Cruise

 Which 1980s sitcom star is married to *Game of Thrones* actor Jason Momoa?

- Tatyana Ali
- Lisa Bonet
- Keshia Knight Pulliam
- Anna Paquin

ANSWER 170: Lisa Bonet, who acted in *The Cosby Show*

*Ever notice that
'what the hell' is always
the right decision?*

MARILYN MONROE

 171 What was the first film to sweep the Oscars?

- *It Happened One Night*
- *Casablanca*
- *The Wizard of Oz*
- *Gone with the Wind*

ANSWER 171: In 1934, *It Happened One Night* won all five major awards: Best Picture, Best Director, Best Actor, Best Actress, and Best Screenplay.

172 How much did Marilyn Monroe's dress sell for at auction?

- $1.2 million
- $2.4 million
- $3.6 million
- $4.8 million

ANSWER 172: The dress worn by Marilyn Monroe in which she famously crooned 'Happy Birthday, Mr. President,' was sold for $4.8 million.

173 What was Larry Hagman's job in the 1960s sitcom *I Dream of Jeannie*?

- An advertising executive
- An astronaut
- A scientist
- An artist

ANSWER 173: An astronaut

174 Match the actress below with the Jane Austen character she portrayed:

1. Kiera Knightley
2. Emma Thompson
3. Judi Dench
4. Gwyneth Paltrow

A. Lady Catherine, in *Pride and Prejudice*
B. Emma Woodhouse, in *Emma*
C. Elizabeth Bennet, in *Pride and Prejudice*
D. Elinor Dashwood, in *Sense and Sensibility*

175 Who is the voice for Bruce the vegetarian white shark in *Finding Nemo*?

- Robert De Niro
- Barry Humphries
- Anthony Hopkins
- Eddie Murphy

176 Who was the first winner of a Best Actor Oscar to decline it?

- George C. Scott
- Marlon Brando
- Paul Newman
- Will Smith

ANSWER 176: George C. Scott, for 1970's biopic *Patton*, reasoning that dramatic performances were unique to one another and shouldn't be compared

177 How many hours per day did it take makeup artists to turn Ron Perlman into the title character in *Hellboy*?

- Two
- Three
- Four
- Five

People think that the directors direct actors. No. Really, what the director's doing is directing the audience's eye through the film.

JULIANNE MOORE

178 The HBO series *Westworld* is shot on the same set of what iconic comedy film?

- *Three Amigos*
- *Blazing Saddles*
- *Priscilla, Queen of the Desert*
- Laurel and Hardy's *Way Out West*

ANSWER 178: *Blazing Saddles*

179 Match the novelist with the screenplay they are credited with writing:

1. William Faulkner
2. Michael Chabon
3. Joan Didion
4. Cormac McCarthy

A. *Spider-Man 2*
B. *A Star Is Born*
C. *The Counselor*
D. *The Big Sleep*

180 What was Pierce Brosnan contractually forbidden to do from 1995-2002, in any movie that wasn't part of the James Bond franchise?

- Drink a martini
- Wear a tuxedo
- Skydive
- Gamble

181 What kind of bird was Big Bird, of *Sesame Street*?

- Cuckoo
- Chicken
- Canary
- Cassowary

ANSWER 181: Big Bird is an 8'2" canary.

182 How many pairs of glasses did Daniel Radcliffe go through by the end of the Harry Potter series of films?

- 100
- 120
- 160
- 200

183 Frank Capra included what "lucky charm" in all his films from 1938's *You Can't Take It with You* onwards?

- His mother's teapot
- A potted cactus
- A raven
- A small painting of the Blessed Mother

ANSWER 183: His pet raven Jimmy. In *It's A Wonderful Life*, the bird appears in George Bailey's workshop.

201

 184 Who was the first cast member hired on *Saturday Night Live*?

- Chevy Chase
- Bill Murray
- Gilda Radner
- John Belushi

ANSWER 184: Gilda Radner

In my view, the only way to see a film remains the way the filmmaker intended: inside a large movie theater with great sound and pristine picture.

RIDLEY SCOTT

185 The first makeup designed specifically for movies was called Supreme Greasepaint, developed in 1914 by what company?

- Max Factor
- Avon
- Sears Roebuck
- Revlon

186 Match the name of the actress below with her original name:

1. Whoopi Goldberg
2. Marilyn Monroe
3. Queen Latifah
4. Portia de Rossi

A. Dana Owens
B. Amanda Lee Rogers
C. Caryn Johnson
D. Norma Jean Baker

187 How many films did Spencer Tracy and Katharine Hepburn make together?

- Five
- Seven
- Nine
- Eleven

188 Who was the first major American director to shoot a movie in the People's Republic of China?

- Steven Spielberg
- Ridley Scott
- Francis Ford Coppola
- Rob Reiner

189 What is the name of the television program on *Home Improvement* fronted by Tim Taylor, played by Tim Allen?

- *This Old House*
- *Tool Time*
- *How to Fix It*
- *Power Tool Hour*

190 What did Hitchcock use for blood in *Psycho*?

- Corn syrup
- Chocolate syrup
- Vegetable oil
- Motor oil

ANSWER 190: Because he was filming in black and white, he used chocolate syrup.

209

191 Whose brain made a cameo x-ray appearance during an episode of the forensic drama *Bones*?

- Albert Einstein
- Elmer Fudd
- Charles Manson
- Homer Simpson

*I was a ballerina,
but I had to quit after
I injured a groin muscle.
It wasn't mine.*

RITA RUDNER

192 Who is the first American actress to play a Bond girl in the James Bond series?

- Ann Margaret
- Angie Dickenson
- Leslie Caron
- Jill St. John

ANSWER 192: Jill St. John, who played Tiffany Case in *Diamonds Are Forever* in 1971

193 Movies featuring young female protagonists struggling for love and romance are termed 'chick flicks,' and are often released around what time of the year?

- Thanksgiving
- Christmas
- Valentine's Day
- Midsummer

194 What children's movie did famed James Bond producer Albert Broccoli make?

- *Mary Poppins*
- *Mr. Popper's Penguins*
- *Swiss Family Robinson*
- *Chitty Chitty Bang Bang*

195 Who created the distinctively high falsetto of Mickey Mouse?

- Mel Blanc
- Walt Disney
- Fritz Freleng
- Tex Avery

ANSWER 195: Walt Disney himself voiced the character Mickey Mouse from the character's inception in 1929 until 1946, when executive duties left little time for voice acting.

215

196 How many eggs does Paul Newman's character eat in *Cool Hand Luke*?

- Twenty
- Thirty
- Forty
- Fifty

197 Which nightly news anchor always ended his broadcasts with "And that's the way it is . . . "?

- Tom Brokaw
- David Brinkley
- Walter Cronkite
- Dan Rather

198 Who was the most highly paid actor of 2017?

- Mark Wahlberg
- Tom Cruise
- Vin Diesel
- Adam Sandler

ANSWER 198: Mark Wahlberg, who made $68 million from endorsements, investments, and acting

My experience with casting children is that . . . the whole movie is going to rest on their shoulders, so you have to set aside time and wait for the perfect people to appear.

WES ANDERSON

199 How many times does
The Dude in *The Big Lebowski*
say "man" during the course
of the film?

- 15
- 80
- 147
- 421

200 Match the film with its tagline:

1. *Brokeback Mountain*

2. *Fargo*

3. *Jurassic Park*

4. *The 40-Year-Old Virgin*

A. A lot can happen in the middle of nowhere.

B. An adventure 65 million years in the making.

C. The longer you wait, the harder it gets.

D. Love is a force of nature.

201 Who was the youngest actress to be nominated for Best Actress?

- Ellen Page
- Keisha Castle-Hughes
- Anna Paquin
- Keira Knightley

ANSWER 201: Keisha Castle-Hughes was thirteen when she was nominated for an Oscar for her work in *The Whale Rider*, set in New Zealand.

202 What Academy Award was presented the first year of the Oscars. But never again?

- Best Stunt Work
- Best Title Writing
- Best Casting
- Best Movie Trailer

ANSWER 202: Best Title Writing (an award for silent films) was awarded to Joseph Farnham at the 1st Academy Awards. He was awarded for his work that year on four films.

THE END